This publication provides general information on Employer Identification Numbers (EINs). The topics included are:

- *What is an EIN*
- *Information by type of business entity*
- *When you need a new EIN*
- *How to apply for an EIN*
- *How to complete Form SS-4*
- *Where to apply for an EIN*
- *How to avoid common problems*

I0475121

Table of Contents

What is an EIN?

An Employer Identification Number (EIN) is a nine-digit number that IRS assigns in the following format: XX-XXXXXXX. It is used to identify the tax accounts of employers and certain others who have no employees. However, for employee plans, an alpha (for example, P) or the plan number (e.g., 003) may follow the EIN. The IRS uses the number to identify taxpayers that are required to file various business tax returns. EINs are used by employers, sole proprietors, corporations, partnerships, non-profit associations, trusts, estates of decedents, government agencies, certain individuals, and other business entities. Use your EIN on all of the items that you send to the IRS and the Social Security Administration (SSA).

Caution: An EIN is for use in connection with your business activities only. Do not use your EIN in place of your social security number (SSN).

Effective May 21, 2012, to ensure fair and equitable treatment for all taxpayers, the Internal Revenue Service will limit Employer Identification Number (EIN) issuance to one per responsible party per day. This limitation is applicable to all requests for EINs whether online or by fax or mail. We apologize for any inconvenience this may cause.

You should have only one EIN for the same business entity. If you have more than one EIN and are not sure which one to use, call the Business and Specialty Tax Line at 1-800-829-4933 (TTY/TDD users can call 1-800-829-4059). Provide the numbers that you have, the name and address to which each was assigned, and the address of your main place of business. The IRS will tell you which number to use.

If you do not have your EIN by the time your return is due, write "Applied For" and the date that you applied for it in the space shown for the number.

Special Rules Regarding Entity Classification Elections

There are special rules and procedures for classification elections made on Form 8832, Entity Classification Election. Those rules and procedures are not reflected in this publication. The results explained in this publication may be different when an entity classification election is involved. See the instructions for Form 8832 for further information regarding entity classification elections.

Information by Type of Business Entity

This section contains the following information:

- Definitions of various entity types
- Which forms each entity type may file
- When you need a new EIN
- When you don't need a new EIN

Sole Proprietorship

Definition

A sole proprietorship is an unincorporated business that is owned by one individual. It is the simplest form of business organization to start and maintain. The business has no existence apart from you, the owner. Its liabilities are your personal liabilities and you undertake the risks of the business for all assets owned, whether or not used in the business. Include the income and expenses of the business on your own tax return. For more information on sole proprietorships, see Publication 334, Tax Guide for Small Businesses. If you are a farmer, see Publication 225, Farmer's Tax Guide.

Form(s):

Business profits or losses of a sole proprietorship are reported on Schedule C, Schedule C-EZ, or Schedule F of Form 1040, U.S. Individual Income Tax Return. A sole proprietor may also be required to file other returns (such as employment or excise tax returns).

You will need a new EIN if any of the following are true:

- You file bankruptcy under Chapter 7 (liquidation) or Chapter 11 (reorganization) of the Bankruptcy Code

- You incorporate

- You are a sole proprietor and take in partners and operate as a partnership

- You are establishing a pension, profit sharing, or retirement plan

You do not need a new EIN if any of the following are true:

- You change the name of your business

- You change your location or add locations (stores, plants, enterprises or branches of the entity)

- You operate multiple businesses (including stores, plants, enterprises or branches of the entity)

  Note: If you are a sole proprietor who conducts business as a limited liability company (LLC), you do not need a separate EIN for the LLC, unless you are required to file employment or excise tax returns. A limited liability company is an entity formed under state law by filing articles of organization as an LLC. An LLC owned by one individual is automatically treated as a sole proprietorship for federal income tax purposes (referred to as an entity to be disregarded as separate from its owner). Report the business activities of the LLC on your Form 1040 using a Schedule C, Schedule C-EZ or Schedule F.

Corporation

Definition:

A corporation is defined as a legal entity or structure created under the authority of the laws of a state consisting of a person, or group of persons, who become
shareholders. The entity's existence is considered separate and distinct from that of
its members. Since a corporation is an entity in its own right, it is liable for its own
debts and obligations. In forming a corporation, prospective shareholders transfer
money, property, or both, for the corporation's capital stock.

The following businesses formed after 1996 are taxed as corporations:

- A business formed under a federal or state law that refers to it as a corporation,
  body corporate, or body politic

- A business formed under a state law that refers to it as a joint-stock company or
  joint-stock association

- An insurance company

- Certain banks

- A business wholly owned by a state or local government

- A business specifically required to be taxed as a corporation by the
  Internal Revenue Code

- Certain foreign businesses

- Any other business that elects to be taxed as a corporation. For example, a limited
  liability company (LLC) by filing Form 8832, Entity Classification Election. For
  more information, see the instructions for Form 8832.

Form(s):

Corporations usually file a Form 1120 series return, plus other returns that apply
(such as employment or excise tax returns).

The Form 1120 series returns are as follows:

- Form 1118, Foreign Tax Credit-Corporation

- Form 1120, U.S. Corporation Income Tax Return

- Form 1120-C, U.S. Income Tax Return for Cooperative Associations

- Form 1120-F, U.S. Income Tax Return of a Foreign Corporation

- Form 1120-FSC, U.S. Income Tax Return of a Foreign Sales Corporation

- Form 1120-H, U.S. Income Tax Return for Homeowners Associations

- Form 1120-L, U.S. Life Insurance Company Income Tax Return

- Form 1120-ND, Return for Nuclear Decommissioning Funds and Certain Related
  Persons

- Form 1120-PC, U.S. Property and Casualty Insurance Company Income Tax
  Return

- Form 1120-POL, U.S. Income Tax Return for Certain Political Organizations

- Form 1120-REIT, U.S. Income Tax Return for Real Estate Investment Trusts

- Form 1120-RIC, U.S. Income Tax Return for Regulated Investment Companies

- Form 1120S, U.S. Income Tax Return for an S Corporation

- Form 1120-SF, U.S. Income Tax Return for Designated Settlement Funds (Under section 468B)

- Form 1120-W, Estimated Tax for Corporations

- Form 1120-X, Amended U.S. Corporation Income Tax Return

You will need a new EIN if any of the following are true:
- You are a subsidiary of a corporation and currently use the parent's corporate EIN

- You become a subsidiary of a corporation

- The corporation becomes a partnership or a sole proprietorship

- You create a new corporation after a statutory merger

- You receive a new corporate charter

You will not need a new EIN if any of the following are true:
- You are a division of a corporation

- After a corporate merger, the surviving corporation uses its existing EIN

- A corporation declares bankruptcy. However, if a liquidating trust is established for a corporation that is in bankruptcy, an EIN for that trust is required. See Treasury Reg. § 301.7701-4(d).

- Your business name changes

- You change your location or add locations (stores, plants, enterprises or branches)

- You elect to be taxed as an S Corporation by filing Form 2553

- After a corporate reorganization, you only change identity, form, or place of organization

- The corporation is sold and the assets, liabilities and charters are obtained by the buyer

Partnership

Definition:
A partnership is the relationship existing between two or more persons who join together to carry on a trade or business. Each partner contributes money, property, labor or skill, and expects to share in the profits and losses of the business.

The term 'partnership' includes a limited partnership, syndicate, group, pool, joint venture, or other unincorporated organization, through or by which any business, financial operation, or venture is carried on.

An unincorporated organization with two or more members is generally classified as a partnership for federal tax purposes if its members carry on a trade, business, financial operation, or venture and divide its profits. However, a joint undertaking merely to share expenses is not a partnership. For example, co-ownership of property maintained and rented or leased is not a partnership unless the co-owners provide services to the tenants.

Husband and Wife Businesses – Sole Proprietorship or Partnership?

Many small businesses are operated by husband and wife, without incorporating or creating a formal partnership agreement. A husband and wife business may be a partnership, whether or not a formal partnership agreement is made. However, see the information below regarding legislation designed to reduce taxpayer burden for husband and wife businesses.

The Small Business and Work Opportunity Tax Act of 2007 (Public Law 110-28) provides that for tax years beginning after December 31, 2006, a qualified joint venture conducted by a husband and wife who file a joint return is not rated as a partnership for federal tax purposes. A qualified joint venture, for purposes of this provision, includes only businesses that are owned and operated by spouses as co-owners, and not in the name of a state law entity (including a general or limited liability company).

If a husband and wife materially participate as the only members of a jointly owned and operated business, and file a joint federal income tax return (Form 1040), they can elect for the business to be taxed as a qualified joint venture instead of a partnership. To make the election, all items of income, gain, loss, deduction, and credit must be divided between the spouses, in accordance with each spouse's interests in the venture, and reported on separate Schedules C or F as sole proprietors.

Spouses who meet these qualifications and require EINs should submit separate Forms SS-4 as sole proprietors. Do not apply for a joint EIN as a "Qualified Joint Venture".

> *Note:* If your spouse is your employee, not your partner, you must pay Social Security and Medicare taxes for him or her.

Form(s):

A partnership files Form 1065, U.S. Partnership Return of Income, plus other returns that apply (such as employment or excise tax returns).

You will need a new EIN if any of the following are true:

- You incorporate
- One partner takes over and operates as a sole proprietorship
- The partnership is terminated (no part of any business, financial operation, or venture of the partnership continues to be carried on by any of its partners in a partnership) and a new partnership is begun

You do not need a new EIN if any of the following are true:

- The partnership declares bankruptcy. However, if a liquidating trust is established for a partnership that is in bankruptcy, an EIN for that trust is required. See Treasury Reg. § 301.7701-4(d)
- The partnership name changes
- The location of the partnership changes or new locations are added.
- The partnership terminates under IRC Section 708(b)(1)(B). A partnership shall be considered terminated if within a 12-month period there is a sale or exchange of at least 50% of the total interest in partnership capital and profits to another partner. If the purchaser and remaining partners immediately contribute the properties to a new partnership, they can retain the old partnership EIN.

Estate

Definitions:

Estate: An estate is a legal entity created as the result of a person's death. The decedent's estate is a separate legal entity for federal tax purposes. An estate consists of real and/or personal property of the deceased person. The estate pays any debts owed by the decedent and then distributes the balance of the estate's assets to the beneficiaries of the estate. The estate exists until the final distribution of the assets is made to the heirs and other beneficiaries.

Fiduciary: A fiduciary is any person acting in a fiduciary capacity for any other person. A fiduciary for a decedent's estate can be an executor, administrator, personal representative, or person in possession of property of a decedent's estate. The primary duties of the fiduciary are to collect all the decedent's assets, pay the creditors, and distribute the remaining assets to the heirs or other beneficiaries.

Form(s):

- Estates file either Form 706, United States Estate (and Generation-Skipping Transfer) Tax Return, or
- Form 1041, U.S. Fiduciary Return of Income, plus other returns that apply (such as employment or excise tax returns)

You will need a new EIN if any of the following are true:

- A trust is created with estate funds. Such a trust is not simply a continuation of the estate.
- You represent an estate that operates a business after the owner's death.

You will not need a new EIN if any of the following are true:

- The administrator, personal representative, or executor changes
- The beneficiaries of an estate change

Trust

Definitions

Trust: A trust is an arrangement through which trustees take title to property for the purpose of protecting or conserving it for the beneficiaries under the ordinary rules applied in chancery or probate courts. A trust is a legal entity created under state law and taxed under federal law. A trust may be created during an individual's lifetime (inter vivos) or at the time of his or her death under a will (testamentary). Trusts include guardianships, custodianships, conservatorships, receiverships, escrow accounts, Ginnie Mae (GNMA) and Fannie Mae (FNMA) pools.

Fiduciary/Trustee: A fiduciary is an individual or organization charged with the duty to act for the benefit of another. A trustee is a fiduciary. The trustee obtains legal title to the trust assets and is required to administer the trust on behalf of the beneficiaries according to the express terms and provisions of the trust agreement.

Beneficiary: A beneficiary is a person designated as a recipient of funds or other property under a trust or an estate.

Grantor: The grantor (also known as trustor, settlor, or creator) is the creator of the trust relationship and is generally the owner of the assets initially contributed to the trust. The grantor generally establishes, in the trust instrument, the terms and provisions of the trust relationship between the grantor, the trustee, and the beneficiary. The grantor may retain control over all or a portion of the trust, which may result in the grantor being subject to tax on the income from that portion of the trust.

Revocable/Irrevocable Trust: An irrevocable trust is a trust, which, by its terms, cannot be modified, amended, or revoked. For tax purposes, an irrevocable trust can be treated as a simple, complex, or grantor trust, depending on the powers listed in the trust instrument. A revocable trust may be revoked and is considered a grantor trust (IRC § 676). State law and the trust instrument establish whether a trust is revocable or irrevocable. If the trust instrument is silent on revocability, then most states consider the trust revocable.

Living Trust: A living person creates an inter vivos trust during that person's lifetime. An inter vivos trust can be established as revocable or irrevocable. An inter vivos trust can be a simple, complex, or grantor trust depending on the trust instrument.

Testamentary Trust: A testamentary trust is created by a will, which begins its existence upon the death of the person making the will, when property is transferred from the decedent's estate. Testamentary trusts are generally simple or complex trusts. A testamentary trust is irrevocable by definition, as it comes into being at the death of the grantor. A "trust under the will' is the same as a testamentary trust.

Conservatorship: A trust, not an estate, which is usually set up for an incompetent person.

Guardianship/Custodianship: A trust usually set up for a minor.

Form(s):

Form 1041 U.S. Fiduciary Return of Income, plus other returns that apply (such as employment tax returns).

You will need a new EIN if any of the following are true:

- A trust changes to an estate
- A living (inter vivos) trust changes to a testamentary trust
- The revocable trust changes to an irrevocable trust

You will not need a new EIN if any of the following are true:

- The trustee changes
- The grantor or beneficiary changes his or her name or address.

  Note: Separate EINs are needed if one person is the grantor/maker of multiple trusts. For example, if you have a trust for each of your grandchildren, each trust must have a separate EIN and file a separate tax return. However, a single trust with several beneficiaries requires only one EIN.

Employee Plans

Definitions:

Employee Benefit Plan: An employee benefit plan is a permanent arrangement under which an employer provides retirement or health benefits for employees. Some of these include: cafeteria plans, defined benefit plans, and defined contribution plans. The employer/sponsor and/or the plan administrator file the applicable returns.

Plan Sponsor: The plan sponsor is the entity that establishes and maintains a benefits plan. The plan sponsor is usually an employer, but may also be an employee organization created for the purpose of offering benefits. If the plan is a "multi-employer plan," the committee or other entity that established the plan is considered the plan sponsor.

Plan Administrator: The plan administrator is the person or company who handles day-to-day details of operating a health benefit or pension plan, such as processing claims for benefits, employer and employee contributions, record-keeping, and reports. The administrator is usually identified in the plan creation documents.

Note: If you are reporting withholding on pension distributions, be sure to be consistent in using the same name and EIN for all reporting and depositing of taxes, i.e. Forms 945, 1099-R, and 8109/EFTPS. Filing Form 945 with an incorrect name or EIN or failure to use the same name and EIN in all reporting and depositing of taxes may result in penalties and delays in processing your return.

Form(s):

Employee plans usually file Form 5500 series returns plus other returns that apply (such as employment or excise taxes). The major employee plan forms are listed below.

Note: If the employer/sponsor entity already has an EIN, use that number on all Form 5500 series returns.

- (electronic) Form 5500-SF, Short Form Annual Return/Report of Small Benefit Plan

- Form 5500-C/R, Return/Report of Employee Benefit Plan (with fewer than 100 participants)

- Form 5500-EZ, Annual Return of One-Participant (Owners and Their Spouses) Pension Benefit Plan

- Form 1099-R, Distributions From Pensions, Annuities, Retirement or Profit-Sharing Plans, IRAs, Insurance Contracts, etc.

- Form 5304-SIMPLE, Savings Incentive Match Plan for Employees of Small Employers (SIMPLE) (Not Subject to the Designated Financial Institution Rules)

- Form 5305-SEP, Simplified Employee Pension-Individual Retirement Accounts Contribution Agreement

- Form 5305A-SEP, Salary Reduction and Other Elective Simplified Employee Pension-Individual Retirement Accounts Contribution Agreement

- Form 5305-SIMPLE, Savings Incentive Match Plan for Employees of Small

Employers (SIMPLE) (for Use With a Designated Financial Institution)

- Form 5329, Additional Taxes Attributable to IRAs, Other Qualified Retirement Plans, Annuities, Modified Endowment Contracts, and MSAs
- Form 5330, Return of Excise Taxes Related to Employee Benefit Plans

    Note: For more information on employee plans, visit the Retirement Plans Community located on the IRS website at **www.irs.gov**, or call 1-800-TAX FORM, and ask for Package 5500.

Exempt Organizations

Definitions:

Tax Exempt Organization: A tax exempt organization is a non-profit organization that is exempt from certain taxes because it is described under Section 501 of the Internal Revenue Code. Certain organizations are required to apply to the Internal Revenue Service for a determination letter that grants them formal tax exemption, while other organizations are treated as tax exempt as long as they are organized and operated under an applicable section of the Code.

IRC Section 501(c)(3) Organization: This is an organization that is organized and operated exclusively for one or more of the following purposes: charitable, religious, educational, scientific, literary, testing for public safety, fostering national or international amateur sports competition (but only if none of its activities involve providing athletic facilities or equipment), or the prevention of cruelty to animals. To qualify, the organization must be a corporation, community chest, fund, unincorporated association, or foundation. A trust is a fund or foundation and will qualify. However, an individual or a partnership will not qualify.

Organizations not required to apply for formal tax exempt status: Some organizations are treated as tax exempt under IRC Section 501(c)(3) without being required to file Form 1023, provided they are organized and operated appropriately. These include:

- Churches, interchurch organizations of local units of a church, conventions or associations of churches, or integrated auxiliaries of a church, such as a men's or women's organization, religious school, mission society, or youth group.
- Any organization (other than a private foundation) normally having annual gross-receipts of not more than $5,000.

Contributions to domestic 501(c)(3) organizations, except organizations testing for public safety, are generally deductible as charitable contributions on the donor's federal income tax return.

Private Foundation vs. Public Charity: Most organizations that are exempt from income tax under IRC Section 501(c)(3) are presumed to be private foundations, unless they notify the Internal Revenue Service within a specified period of time that they are not. In effect, the definition divides organizations into two classes, namely private foundations and public charities. There is an excise tax on the net investment income of most domestic private foundations. In addition, there are several other rules that apply.

See Publication 557 for a chart listing many other categories of exempt organizations.

Organizations seeking formal recognition of their exempt status must generally file one of the applications listed below with the Internal Revenue Service and must pay the required user fee. Requests for exemption under subsections other than 501(c)(3) must include Form 8718, User Fee for Exempt Organization Determination Letter Request. Requests should be sent to the address shown on Form 1023 and on Form 8718. To decide which application form listed below is needed for your organization, refer to Publication 557, Tax-Exempt Status for Your Organization.

- Form 1023, Application for Recognition of Exemption Under Section 501(c)(3) of the Internal Revenue Code

- Form 1024, Application for Recognition of Exemption Under Section 501(a) for Determination Under Section 120 of the Internal Revenue Code

  Note: All non-profit organizations must apply for an EIN before filing for exempt status.

All publications and forms mentioned above are available for download from the IRS website, **www.irs.gov**, or by calling our toll-free number 1-800-TAX-FORM.

Group Exemption Letter: A group exemption letter is a ruling or determination letter issued to a central organization recognizing, on a group basis, the exemption of subordinate organizations on whose behalf the central organization has applied for recognition of exemption. A central organization is an organization that has one or more subordinates under its control. A subordinate organization is a chapter, local, post, or unit of a central organization.

Public Disclosure of Forms 990: Exempt organization Forms 990 are required to be made available to the public. Procedures for obtaining this information are found in Publication 557, Tax-Exempt Status for Your Organization, and Form 4506A, Request for Public Inspection or Copy of Exempt or Political Organization. In addition, submitted Forms 990-N are made available on the IRS website, www.irs.gov.

Unrelated Business Income: Even though an organization is recognized as tax-exempt, it still may be liable for tax on its unrelated business income. Unrelated business income is income from a trade or business, regularly carried on, that is not substantially related to the charitable, educational, or other purpose that is the basis for the organization's exemption.

Form(s)

Exempt organizations usually file a Form 990 series return plus other returns that apply (such as employment or excise tax returns). The exempt organization forms are listed below:

- Form 990-N, e-Postcard

- Form 990, Return of Organizations Exempt From Income Tax

- Form 990-EZ, Short Form Return of Organization Exempt From Income Tax

- Form 990-BL, Information and Initial Excise Tax Return for Black Lung Benefit Trusts and Certain Related Persons

- Form 990-PF, Return of Private Foundation or Section 4947(a)(1) Charitable Trusts Treated as a Private Foundation

- Form 990-T, Exempt Organization Business Income Tax Return

- Form 4720, Return of Certain Excise Taxes on Charities and Other Persons under Chapters 41 and 42 of the Internal Revenue Code

- Form 5578, Annual Certification of Racial Nondiscrimination for a Private School Exempt from Federal Income Tax

Annual information returns: Except for private foundations, which must file Form 990-PF annually regardless of gross receipts, an exempt organization that normally has $25,000 or more in gross receipts must file an exempt organization information return Form 990, Return of Organization Exempt from Income Tax, whether or not the organization has formal tax exempt status. Most organizations not required to file a Form 990/Form 990-EZ or Form 990-PF are required to submit a Form 990-N, e-Postcard, for tax years that began after December 31, 2006. Organizations exempted from this requirement are listed in Publication 557, Tax Exempt Status for Your Organization. Special filing rules apply to supporting organizations described in IRC section 509(a)(3). These rules can also be found in Publication 557.

Limited Liability Company (LLC)

Definition: A limited liability company (LLC) is an entity formed under state or foreign law by filing articles of organization as an LLC. Unlike a partnership, none of the members of an LLC are personally liable for its debts.

LLC Tax Classification: Treas. Reg. Section 301.7701-3 provides guidance on classification for limited liability companies. Generally, if the business is an unincorporated business entity, and there are two or more owners, the entity can choose to be a partnership or a corporation. If an unincorporated business entity has only one owner, it can either elect to be a corporation or the entity can be disregarded. If an individual owns a disregarded entity, it is treated as a sole proprietorship. If a corporation owns a disregarded entity, it is treated as a division or branch of the corporation. See Form 8832, Entity Classification Election, for more details.

> *Note:* While a single member entity, that does not elect corporate status, will default to a disregarded status for some federal tax purposes, it will not be disregarded for all federal tax purposes. For federal employment taxes (after January 1, 2009) and certain excise taxes (after January 1, 2008) it will be treated as a separate entity.

Single Member LLC:

A single member LLC generally has the following choices:

(1) File Form 8832 to be taxed as a corporation

(2) If qualified, file Form 2553, Election by a Small Business Corporation (Under Section 1362 of the Internal Revenue Code), to be taxed as an S corporation

(3) Be taxed (by default) as a disregarded entity

- If the single member is an individual, the LLC will be taxed as a sole proprietorship

- If the single member is a business entity, the LLC will be taxed as a division of the corporation

Multiple Member LLC:

A multiple member LLC generally has the following choices:

(1) File Form 8832 to be taxed as a corporation

(2) If qualified, file Form 2553 to be taxed as an S-Corporation

(3) Be taxed (by default) as a partnership

Note: A husband and wife, who are owners of an LLC, and share in the profits of such, can file as a single member if they reside in a Community Property State (Arizona, California, Idaho, Louisiana, New Mexico, Nevada, Texas, Washington, or Wisconsin). Publication 555, Community Property, contains additional information on Community Property laws.

If you are organized as a limited liability company and require an EIN, please refer to the instructions for Form SS-4 for information on completing the form or apply online using the Internet EIN application available at www.irs.gov and select "Limited Liability Company" as the type of entity you are establishing.

Employment and Excise Taxes

Employment Taxes

Definition:

If you have one or more employees, you will generally be required to withhold federal income tax from their wages. You also may be subject to social security and Medicare taxes under the Federal Insurance Contributions Act (FICA) and federal unemployment tax under the Federal Unemployment Tax Act (FUTA).

If you are required to report employment taxes or give tax statements to employees or annuitants, you need an employer identification number (EIN).

Form(s):

Social security, Medicare, and withheld income tax are usually reported on Form 941, Employer's QUARTERLY Federal Tax Return. The exceptions are:

- If your employees are agricultural workers, file Form 943, Employer's Annual Tax Return for Agricultural Employees.

- If your yearly employment taxes will be $1,000 or less (average annual wages of $4,000 or less) you may file Form 944, Employer's ANNUAL Federal Tax Return, rather than Form 941, Employer's QUARTERLY Federal Tax Return. Do not file Form 944 unless the IRS has notified you of this requirement.

- If your employee(s) does household work in your private, non-farm home (for example, child care, housekeeping, or gardening work) attach Schedule H, Household Employment Taxes, to your Form 1040.

  Note: Employers must report and pay required employment taxes for household domestic employees on Schedule H attached to Forms 1040 or 1040A. While withheld amounts no longer have to be deposited on a monthly basis, employers do need an employer identification number (EIN) to include on Form W-2 and Schedule H.

Non-payroll items, including backup withholding and withholding for pensions, annuities, IRAs, and gambling winnings are reported on Form 945, Annual Return of Withheld Federal Income Tax. The return is due January 31 of the following year.

Report Federal Unemployment Tax on Form 940, Employer's Annual Federal Unemployment (FUTA) Tax Return.

Excise Taxes

Definition:

Excise tax is a tax on the manufacture, sale, or consumption of a specific commodity. Examples are: fuel taxes, environmental taxes, and communications and air transportation taxes.

Form(s):

Most excise taxes are reported on Form 720, Quarterly Federal Excise Tax Return. Certain excise taxes are reported on different forms and to other organizations. Those excise taxes and forms are:

- Form 2290, Highway Use Tax

- Form 730, Tax on Wagering

- Form 11-C, Occupational Tax Return and Application for Registry-Wagering

- TTB Form 5300.26, Firearms and Ammunition Excise Tax Return, and Special Tax Registration and Return, TTB Form 5630.5

How to Apply for an EIN

You can apply for an EIN online, by fax, or mail depending on how soon you need to use the EIN

Apply Online

Note: This is a free service offered by the Internal Revenue Service at **www.irs.gov**. Beware of websites on the internet that charge for this free service.

The internet is the preferred method to use when applying for an EIN. Visit the IRS website at **www.irs.gov** (keyword "EIN") and check out the Interview-style online EIN application. The application includes embedded help topics and hyperlinked keywords and definitions so separate instructions aren't needed. The information you submit is validated during the online session. Once you've completed the application, you will receive your EIN immediately. You can then download, save, and print your confirmation notice. (This feature is not available to Third Party Designees.) The online application is fast, free, and user-friendly!

The application is available during the following hours:

Monday - Friday 7:00 a.m. to 10:00 p.m. Eastern time

The online application is available for all entities whose principal business, office or agency, or legal residence (in the case of an individual), is located in the United States or U.S. Territories. Additionally, the principal officer, general partner, grantor, owner, trustor etc. must have a valid Taxpayer Identification Number (Social Security Number, Employer Identification Number, or Individual Taxpayer Identification Number) in order to use the online application.

Apply by Fax

You can receive your EIN by fax within four (4) business days. Fax your completed Form SS-4 to the fax number listed for your state under "Where to Apply" in this publication. The fax number is available 24 hours a day, 7 days a week. Be sure to provide your fax number so that an IRS representative can fax the EIN back to you. Do not fax an application and also call the EIN toll-free number for the same entity because a duplicate EIN may be assigned. By using this method, you are authorizing IRS to fax your EIN without a cover sheet.

Apply by Mail

You can receive your EIN by mail within about four (4) weeks. Ensure that the Form SS-4 contains all of the required information and mail the application to the address listed under "Where to Apply" in this publication. An EIN will be assigned and mailed to you.

How to Complete Form SS-4, Application for an EIN

If you choose to apply online, you will not need a Form SS-4. Otherwise, you can download Form SS-4 and separate instructions by accessing the IRS website at **www.irs.gov** or call 1-800-TAX-FORM to request the form and instructions by mail. You can also visit your local IRS office.

Special Characters In Your Business Name:

The only special characters IRS systems can accept in a business name are: 1) alpha (A-Z), 2) numeric (0-9), 3) hyphen (-) and 4) ampersand (&). If the legal name of your business includes anything other than those listed above, you will need to decide how best to enter your business name into the online EIN application or on Form SS-4.

If your legal name contains a symbol or character such as a "plus" symbol (+) or a period (.) you could spell out the symbol and leave a space. Jones.com could be submitted as Jones Dot Com or Jones Com. The backward (\) or forward (/) slash can be substituted with a hyphen (-). If your business name contains an apostrophe ('), drop the apostrophe and do not leave a space.

Third Party Designee:

No matter what method you use to apply, if a third party is making the application for an EIN, the taxpayer must authorize the third party to apply for and receive the EIN.

- A Third Party Designee (TPD) must complete his/her identifying information at the bottom of the Form SS-4.

- The Form SS-4 must be signed by the taxpayer for the TPD authorization to be valid.

- The Form SS-4 must be mailed or faxed to the appropriate Internal Revenue Service campus. See "Where to Apply" in this publication.

The designee's authority terminates at the time the EIN is assigned and released to the designee.

Read the instructions for Form SS-4.

After reading the instructions, find your entity type (sole proprietor, corporation, partnership, etc.).

> *Note:* This is not an election for a tax classification. See Form 8832, Entity Classification Election, for tax classification information.

The Internal Revenue Service has become aware that nominee individuals are being listed as principal officers, general partners, grantors, owners, and trustors in the Employer Identification Number (EIN) application process. A nominee is not one of these people. Rather, nominees are temporarily authorized to act on behalf of entities during the formation process. The use of nominees in the EIN application process prevents the IRS from gathering appropriate information on entity ownership, and has been found to facilitate tax non-compliance by entities and their owners.

The IRS does not authorize the use of nominees to obtain EINs. All EIN applications (mail, fax, phone, electronic) must disclose the name and Taxpayer Identification Number (SSN, ITIN, or EIN) of the true principal officer, general partner, grantor, owner or trustor. This individual or entity, which the IRS will call the "responsible party," controls, manages, or directs the applicant entity and the disposition of its funds and assets.

Follow the line-by-line instructions below to complete Form SS-4 for your entity type.

Sole Proprietor/Individual

Line 1	Enter your first name, middle initial and last name exactly as it appears on your social security card. Do not use abbreviations or nicknames. Do not enter your business name on line 1.
Line 2	Enter your trade name or "doing business as" name, if any.
Line 3	If you have a person designated to receive all of your IRS correspondence, enter that person's name on this line. Otherwise, leave blank.
Line 4a-b	Enter your mailing address. If Line 3 (Care-Of) is completed, enter the address for the designated person.
Lines 5a-b	Enter the location address only if it is different from Lines 4a-b mailing address. Do not enter a PO Box here.
Line 6	Enter the county and state where your principal business is located.
Line 7a-b	N/A
Line 8a	N/A
Line 8b	N/A
Line 8c	N/A
Line 9a	Check the "Sole Proprietor" box and enter your SSN (or ITIN) in the space provided.
Line 9b	N/A

Line 10	Check only one box. If your reason for applying is not specifically listed, check the "Other" box and enter the reason.
Line 11	Enter the date you first started or acquired your business.
Line 12	Enter the last month of your accounting year or tax year (generally December (12) calendar year for a sole proprietor).
Line 13	Enter the highest number of employees expected in the next 12 months (Agricultural, Household or Other). If none, enter 0 and skip to Line 16.
Line 14	If you expect your employment tax liability to be $1,000 or less in a full calendar year and want to file Form 944 annually instead of Forms 941 quarterly check "Yes". (To file Forms 941, check "No".)
Line 15	If your business has (or will have) employees enter the date the business began or will begin to pay wages (Month, Date, Year.) If you have no employees, leave blank. If the applicant is a withholding agent, enter date income will first be paid to nonresident alien.
Line 16	Check the one box that best describes the type of business you operate, i.e. construction, real estate, etc. If none of the boxes apply, check the "Other" box and specify type of business. Do not leave blank or enter "none", or "N/A".
Line 17	Describe the applicant's principal line of business in more detail than Line 16 such as, type of merchandise sold, specific construction product produced or service provided. Do not leave blank or enter "none" or "N/A".
Line 18	If the applicant shown on line one (1) ever applied for and received an EIN previously, check "yes". If "yes", enter previous EIN on the line.

Complete the Third Party Designee section only if you want to authorize the named individual to receive the EIN and answer questions about the completion of Form SS-4. You must also sign the application for the authorization to be valid.

Name and Title: Print your name and title.

Telephone Number: Enter the telephone number where we can reach you if we have questions about your application.

Signature: The sole proprietor must sign the application if the Third Party Designee section is completed.

Corporation

Line 1	Enter the corporate name as it appears on the corporate charter.
Line 2	Enter Doing Business as (DBA) name, only if different from Line 1.
Line 3	If you have a designated person to receive all of your IRS correspondence, enter that person's name on this line. If none, leave blank .
Line 4a-b	Enter your mailing address. If Line 3 (Care-Of) is completed, enter the address for the designated person to receive the tax information.
Lines 5a-b	Enter the business physical location, only if different from Lines 4a-b mailing address. Do not enter a PO Box here.

Line 6   Enter the county and state where principal business is located.

Line 7a   Enter the first name, middle initial, and last name of responsible party. The responsible party will be a president, vice president or other principal officer of the corporation.

Line 7b   Enter the SSN or ITIN of the responsible party shown on Line 7a.

Line 8a   N/A

Line 8b   N/A

Line 9   Check the "Corporation" box, then write on the line the form number that you intend to file (ex: 1120). If you entered "1120S" after the checkbox, you must file Form 2553. See the Instructions for Form 2553.

Line 9b   Enter the state or foreign country where you were incorporated.

Line 10   If your reason for applying is not specifically listed, check the "Other" box and enter the reason.

Line 11   Enter the date you first started or acquired your business.

Line 12   Enter the last month of your accounting year or tax year.

Line 13   Enter the highest number of employees expected in the next 12 months (Agricultural, Household or Other). If none, enter 0 and skip to Line 16.

Line 14   If you expect your employment tax liability to be $1,000 or less in a full calendar year and want to file Form 944 annually instead of Forms 941 quarterly check "Yes". (To file Forms 941, check "No".)

Line 15   If your business has (or will have) employees enter the date the business began or will begin to pay wages (Month, Date, Year). If you have no employees, leave blank. If the applicant is a withholding agent, enter date income will first be paid to nonresident alien.

Line 16   Check one box that best describes the type of business you operate (i.e. construction, real estate, etc..) If none of the listed boxes applies, check the "Other" box and write your specific type of business. Do not leave blank or enter "none" or "N/A".

Line 17   Describe the applicant's principal line of business in more detail (such as, type of merchandise sold, specific construction work, product produced or service provided). Do not leave blank or enter "none" or "N/A".

Line 18   If the applicant shown on line one (1) ever previously applied for and received an EIN, check "yes". If "yes", enter previous EIN on the line.

Complete the Third Party Designee section only if you want to authorize the named individual to receive the EIN and answer questions about the completion of Form SS-4. You must also sign the application for the authorization to be valid.

Name and Title: Print your name and title.

Telephone Number: Enter the telephone number where we can reach you if we have questions about your application.

Signature: The president, vice president, or other principal officer must sign the application if the Third Party Designee section is completed.

Note: If you wish to elect S-corporation status, you must file Form 2553, Election by a Small Business Corporation.

Partnership

Line 1 Enter the name of the partnership as it appears in the partnership agreement.

Line 2 Enter trade name or "doing business as" name, if different from line 1.

Line 3 If you have a person designated to receive all of your IRS correspondence, enter that person's name on this line. If none, leave blank.

Lines 4a-b Enter your mailing address. If Line 3 (Care-Of) is completed, enter the address of the designated person.

Lines 5a-b Enter the business physical location only if different from Lines 4a-b. Do not enter PO Box here.

Line 6 Enter the county and state where principal business is located.

Line 7a Enter the first name, middle initial, last name of the responsible party. The responsible party is a general partner of the partnership.

Line 7b Enter the SSN, ITIN or EIN of the responsible party shown on Line 7a.

Line 8a N/A

Line 8b N/A

Line 8c N/A

Line 9a Check the "Partnership" box.

Line 9b N/A

Line 10 Check only one box. If your reason is not specifically listed, check the "Other" box and enter the reason.

Line 11 Enter the date you first started or acquired your business.

Line 12 Enter the last month of your accounting year or tax year.

Line 13 Enter the highest number of employees expected in the next 12 months (Agricultural, Household or Other). If none, enter 0 and skip to Line 16.

Line 14 If you expect your employment tax liability to be $1,000 or less in a full calendar year and want to file Form 944 annually instead of Forms 941 quarterly check "Yes". (To file Forms 941, check "No".)

Line 15 If your business has (or will have) employees enter the date the business began or will begin to pay wages (Month, Date, Year). If you have no employees leave blank. If the Applicant is a withholding agent, enter date income will first be paid to nonresident alien.

Line 16 Check one box that best describes the type of business you operate (i.e., construction, real estate, etc.). If none of the boxes apply, check the "Other" box and specify type of business. Do not leave blank or enter "none", or "N/A".

Line 17	Describe the applicant's principal line of business in more detail (type of merchandise sold, specific construction work, product produced or service provided). Do not leave blank or enter "none" or "N/A".
Line 18	If the applicant shown on line one (1) ever applied for and received an EIN previously, check "yes". If "yes" enter previous EIN on the line.

Complete the Third Party Designee section only, if you want to authorize the named individual to receive the EIN and answer questions about the completion of Form SS-4. You must also sign the application for the authorization to be valid.

Name and Title: Print your name and title.

Telephone Number: Enter the telephone number where we can reach you if we have questions about your application.

Signature: A responsible and duly authorized member or officer having knowledge of the partnership's affairs must sign the application if the Third Party Designee section is completed.

Trust

Line 1	Enter the exact name of the trust as it appears on the trust instrument.
Line 2	N/A
Line 3	Enter the name of the trustee.
Line 4a-b	Enter mailing address of the trustee, where all IRS correspondence will be mailed.
Lines 5a-b	Enter the physical location of the trustee, only if different from Lines 4a-b mailing address.
Line 6	Enter the county and state where the trust is located.
Line 7a	Enter the name of the responsible party. This will be the grantor, owner or trustor.
Line 7b	Enter the SSN, ITIN or EIN of the person shown on Line 7a.
Line 8a	N/A
Line 8b	N/A
Line 8c	N/A
Line 9a	Check "Trust" and enter the SSN, ITIN, or EIN of the grantor.
Line 9b	N/A
Line 10	Check the "Created a Trust" box.
Line 11	Enter the date the trust was funded.
Line 12	Enter the last month of your accounting year or tax year. Generally, a trust must adopt a calendar year, except for the following trusts: tax-exempt trusts, charitable trusts, and grantor-owned trusts.
Line 13	Enter the highest number of employees expected in the next 12 months (Agricultural, Household or Other). If none, enter 0 and skip to Line 16.

Line 14	If you expect your employment tax liability to be $1,000 or less in a full calendar year and want to file Form 944 annually instead of Forms 941 quarterly check "Yes". (To file Forms 941, check "No".)
Line 15	If your business has (or will have) employees enter the date the business began, or will begin, to pay wages (Month, Date, Year). If you have no employees leave blank. If the applicant is a withholding agent, enter date income will first be paid to nonresident alien.
Line 16	Check the "Finance & Insurance" box.
Line 17	Enter "Trust Administration".
Line 18	If the applicant shown on line one (1) ever applied for and received an EIN previously, check "yes". If "yes", enter previous EIN on the line.

Complete Third Party Designee section only if you want to authorize the named individual to receive the EIN and answer questions about the completion of Form SS-4. You must also sign the application for the authorization to be valid.

Name and Title: Print your name and title.

Telephone Number: Enter the telephone number where we can reach you if we have questions about your application.

Signature: The trustee or other authorized fiduciary must sign the application, if the Third Party Designee section is completed.

GNMA POOLS (Governmental National Mortgage Association)

Note: The EIN Stays with the "GNMA Pool" if it is traded from one financial institution to another.

Line 1	Enter the pool number. Do not enter leading zeros. For example, enter GNMA 00979 as GNMA 979
Line 2	N/A
Line 3	Enter the name of the trustee.
Line 4a-b	Enter the mailing address. This is the address where all IRS correspondence will be sent.
Lines 5a-b	Enter only if different from the mailing address.
Line 6	Enter the county and state where the GNMA Pool is located.
Line 7a-b	N/A
Line 8a	N/A
Line 8b	N/A
Line 8c	N/A
Line 9a	Check "Trust" and enter the TIN of the grantor.
Line 9b	N/A
Line 10	Check the "Other" box and enter "GNMA Pool".

Line 11	Enter the date the "GNMA Pool" was created.
Line 12	Enter 12 for the last month of your accounting year.
Line 13	Enter the highest number of employees expected in the next 12 months (Agricultural, Household or Other). If none, enter 0 and skip to Line 16.
Line 14	If you expect your employment tax liability to be $1,000 or less in a full calendar year and want to file Form 944 annually instead of Forms 941 quarterly check "Yes". (To file Forms 941, check "No".) .
Line 15	If your business has (or will have) employees enter the date the business began or will begin to pay wages (Month, Date, Year). If you have no employees, leave blank.
Line 16	Check the "Finance & Insurance" box.
Line 17	Enter "GNMA".
Line 18	If the applicant entity shown on line one (1) ever applied for and received an EIN previously, check "yes". If "yes", enter previous EIN on the line.

Complete the Third Party Designee section only if you want to authorize the named individual to receive the EIN and answer questions about the completion of this form. You must also sign the application for the authorization to be valid.

Name and Title: Print your name and title of the fiduciary.

Telephone Number: Enter the telephone number where we can reach you if we have questions about your application.

Signature: The trustee or other authorized fiduciary must sign the application if the Third Party Designee Section is completed.

Estate

Line 1	Enter the first name, middle initial and last name of the decedent, followed by "Estate".
Line 2	N/A
Line 3	Enter the name of the executor, administrator, or other fiduciary.
Lines 4a-b	Enter the mailing address. This is the address where all IRS correspondence will be sent.
Lines 5a-b	Enter only if different from the mailing address on Lines 4a-b.
Line 6	Enter the county and state where the will is probated.
Line 7a-b	N/A
Line 8a	N/A
Line 8b	N/A
Line 8c	N/A
Line 9a	Check "Estate" and enter the SSN of the decedent on the line provided.
Line 9b	N/A

Line 10	Check the "Other" box and enter "Estate Administration".
Line 11	Enter the date the estate was funded.
Line 12	Enter the last month of your accounting year or tax year.
Line 13	Enter the highest number of employees expected in the next 12 months (Agricultural, Household or Other). If none, enter 0 and skip to Line 16.
Line 14	If you expect your employment tax liability to be $1,000 or less in a full calendar year and want to file Form 944 annually instead of Forms 941 quarterly check "Yes". (To file Forms 941, check "No".)
Line 15	If the estate has (or will have) employees enter the date the estate will begin to pay wages (Month, Date, Year) If no employees, leave blank.
Line 16	Check the "Finance & Insurance" box.
Line 17	Enter "Estate Administration".
Line 18	If the applicant shown on line one (1) ever previously applied for and received an EIN, check "yes". If "yes" enter previous EIN on the line.

Complete the Third Party Designee section only if you want to authorize the named individual to receive the EIN and answer questions about the completion of this form. You must also sign the application for the authorization to be valid.

Name and Title: Print the name and title of the fiduciary.

Telephone Number: Enter the telephone number where we can reach you if we have questions about your application.

Signature: The fiduciary must sign the application if the Third Party Designee section is completed.

Note: If you use an estate to create a trust, the trust is considered a different entity type and a new EIN is needed.

Plan Administrators

Note: If the plan administrator already has an EIN, use that number. A new EIN is not needed.

Line 1	Enter the name of the plan administrator.
Line 2	N/A
Line 3	If you have a person designated to receive all of your IRS correspondence, enter that person's name on this line. If none, leave blank.
Line 4a-b	Enter the mailing address. This is the address where all IRS correspondence will be sent.
Line 5a-b	Enter only if different from Lines 4a-b mailing address.
Line 6	Enter the county and state where the employee plan is located.
Line 7a-b	N/A
Line 8a	N/A
Line 8b	N/A.

Line 8c	N/A.
Line 9a	Check "Plan Administrator". If the plan administrator is an individual, enter the plan administrator's SSN or ITIN in the space provided. Otherwise enter the EIN.
Line 9b	If you are a corporation, enter the state or foreign country where you were incorporated
Line 10	If your reason is not specifically listed, check the "Other" box and enter the reason.
Line 11	Enter the date you first started or acquired your business.
Line 12	Enter the last month of your accounting year or tax year. Enter the highest number of employees expected in the next 12 months.
Line 13	Enter the highest (Agricultural, Household or Other). If none, enter 0 and skip to Line 16.
Line 14	If you expect your employment tax liability to be $1,000 or less in a full calendar year and want to file Form 944 annually instead of Forms 941 quarterly check "Yes". (To file Forms 941, check "No".)
Line 15	If your business has (or will have) employees enter the date the business began or will begin to pay wages (Month, Date, Year.) If you have no employees leave blank. If the applicant is a withholding agent, enter date income will first be paid to nonresident alien.
Line 16	Check the "Finance & Insurance" box.
Line 17	Enter "Plan Administration".
Line 18	If the applicant shown on line one (1) ever previously applied for and received an EIN, check "yes:. If "yes", enter previous EIN on the line.

Complete the Third Party Designee section only if you want to authorize the named individual to receive the EIN and answer questions about the completion of this form. You must also sign the application for the authorization to be valid.

Name and Title: Print the plan administrator's name and title.

Telephone Number: Enter the telephone number where we can reach you if we have questions about your application.

Signature: A responsible and duly authorized member or officer with the knowledge of plan's affairs must sign if the Third Party Designee section is completed.

Employee Plans

Line 1	Enter the name of the plan.
Line 2	N/A
Line 3	Enter the name of the trustee.
Line 4a-b	Enter the mailing address. This is the address where all IRS correspondence will be sent.
Lines 5a-b	Enter only if different from the mailing address.
Line 6	Enter the county and state where the employee plan is located.

Line 7a-b	Enter the name of responsible party for the plan and SSN, ITIN or EIN.
Line 8a	N/A
Line 8b	N/A
Line 8c	N/A.
Line 9a	Check "Other" and specify "Employee Plan".
Line 9b	N/A
Line 10	Check "Created a Pension Plan".
Line 11	Enter the date you first started or acquired your Employee plan.
Line 12	Enter the last month of your accounting year or tax year.
Line 13	N/A
Line 14	N/A
Line 15	N/A
Line 16	Check the "Finance & Insurance" box.
Line 17	Enter "Employee Plan".
Line 18	If the applicant shown on line one (1) ever previously applied for and received an EIN, check "yes". If "yes", enter previous EIN on the line.

Complete the Third Party Designee section only if you want to authorize the named individual to receive the EIN and answer questions about the completion of this form. You must also sign the application for the authorization to be valid.

Name and Title: Print your name and title.

Telephone Number: Enter the telephone number where we can reach you if we have questions about your application.

Signature: A responsible and duly authorized member or officer with knowledge of the plan's affairs must sign if there is a Third Party Designee.

Exempt Organizations

Line 1	Enter the legal name of the exempt organization.
Line 2	N/A
Line 3	Enter the name of the responsible party for the organization.
Line 4a-b	Enter the mailing address. This is the address where all IRS correspondence will be sent.
Lines 5a-b	Enter only if different from the mailing address in 4a and 4b.
Line 6	Enter the county and state where the exempt organization is located.
Line 7a-b	Enter the name and SSN or ITIN of a responsible and duly authorized member or officer of the exempt organization.
Line 8a	N/A.
Line 8b	N/A

Line 8c	N/A
Line 9a	Check only one box. If you check "other", enter the specific reason for applying.
Line 9b	If you are a corporation, enter the State or Foreign Country where you were incorporated.
Line 10	If your reason is not specifically listed, check the "Other" box and enter the reason.
Line 11	Enter the date you first started or acquired your organization.
Line 12	Enter the last month of your accounting year or tax year.
Line 13	Enter the highest number of employees expected in the next 12 months (Agricultural, Household or Other). If none, enter 0 and skip to Line 16.
Line 14	If you expect your employment tax liability to be $1,000 or less in a full calendar year and want to file Form 944 annually instead of Forms 941 quarterly check "Yes". (To file Forms 941, check "No".)
Line 15	If your business has (or will have) employees enter the date the business began or will begin to pay wages (Month, Date, Year.) If you have no employees, leave blank. If the applicant is a withholding agent, enter date income will first be paid to nonresident alien.
Line 16	Check one box that best describes the type of business you operate (construction, real estate, etc.). If none of the listed boxes apply, check the "Other" box and write your specific type of business. Do not leave blank or enter "none" or "N/A".
Line 17	Describe the applicant's principal line of business in more detail (type of merchandise sold, specific construction work, product produced or service provided). Do not leave blank or enter "none" or "N/A".
Line 18	If the applicant shown on line one (1) ever previously applied for and received an EIN, check "Yes". If "yes", enter previous EIN on the line.

Complete the Third Party Designee section only if you want to authorize the named individual to receive the EIN and answer questions about the completion of this form. You must also sign the application for the authorization to be valid.

Name and Title: Print your name and title.

Telephone Number: Enter the telephone number where we can reach you if we have questions about your application.

Signature: A responsible and duly authorized member or officer having knowledge of the exempt organization's affairs must sign the application if there is a Third Party Designee.

Bankruptcy (Individual)

Bankruptcy proceedings begin with the filing of a petition with the bankruptcy court. The filing of the petition creates a bankruptcy estate, which generally consists of all the assets of the person filing the bankruptcy petition. A separate taxable entity is created if the bankruptcy petition is filed by an individual under Chapter 7 or Chapter 11 of the Bankruptcy Code.

> *Note:* A married couple who file a joint bankruptcy petition require separate EINs for federal tax purposes.

Line 1 Enter the first name, middle initial and last name of the individual who has filed the bankruptcy petition followed by "Bankruptcy Estate".

Line 2 N/A

Line 3 Enter the name of the receiver, debtor in possession, or bankruptcy trustee.

Line 4a-b Enter the trustee or receiver's mailing address.

Line 5a-b Enter only if different from the mailing address.

Line 6 Enter the county and state where the bankruptcy petition was filed.

Line 7a-b Enter the name and SSN (or ITIN) of the bankrupt individual.

Line 8a N/A.

Line 8b N/A.

Line 8c N/A.

Line 9a Check "Other" and write in "individual bankruptcy", "receivership", or "debtor in possession".

Line 9b N/A

Line 10 Check "Other" and write in "bankruptcy", "receivership", or "debtor in possession".

Line 11 Enter the date the bankruptcy estate was created.

Line 12 Enter the last month of your accounting year or tax year.

Line 13 N/A

Line 14 N/A

Line 15 N/A

Line 16 Check the "Other" box and write in "Bankruptcy".

Line 17 Enter "Bankruptcy".

Line 18 If the applicant shown on line one (1) ever previously applied for and received an EIN, check "yes". If "yes", enter previous EIN on the line.

Complete Third Party Designee section only if you want to authorize the named individual to receive the EIN and answer questions about the completion of this form. You must also sign the application for the authorization to be valid.

Name and Title: Print your name and title.

Telephone Number: Enter the telephone number where we can reach you if we have questions about your application.

Signature: The bankruptcy trustee, receiver, or debtor in possession must sign the application if there is a Third Party Designee.

Bankruptcy (Corporation or Partnership)

A separate taxable estate is not created when a partnership or corporation files a bankruptcy petition. The court appointed trustee is, however, responsible for filing the regular income tax returns on Form 1065 or Form 1120.

If you are a bankrupt/liquidated corporation or partnership, you do not need a new EIN. Send the name of the trustee/receiver of the bankruptcy to your IRS service center so we can add that information to your existing EIN account.

EFTPS (Electronic Federal Tax Payment System)

Start your business off right. A Secure Way to Pay All Your Federal Taxes

EFTPS is a tax payment system provided _free_ by the U.S. Department of Treasury. Pay federal taxes electronically - on-line or by phone 24/7. Businesses and Individuals can pay all their federal taxes using EFTPS. Individuals can pay their quarterly 1040ES estimated taxes electronically using EFTPS, and they can make payments weekly, monthly, or quarterly as well as schedule payments for the entire year in advance.

To enroll or for more information online, visit the EFTPS website at **https://www.eftps.gov/eftps/,** or to receive an enrollment form, call EFTPS Customer Service:

* 1-800-555-4477 (for Business payments)
* 1-800-316-6541 (for Individual payments)
* 1-800-733-4829 (TDD Hearing-Impaired)
* 1-800-244-4829 (Español)
* 1-800-555-8778 (EFTPS Online)

Where to Apply for an EIN (Mail or Fax):

If your principal business, office or agency, or legal residence in the case of an individual, is located in:	File or fax with the "Internal Revenue Service Center" at:
One of the 50 states or the District of Columbia	Attn: EIN Operation Cincinnati, OH 45999 Fax-TIN: 859-669-5760
If you have no legal residence, principal place of business, or principal office oragency in any state:	Attn: EIN International Operation Cincinnati, OH 45999 Fax-TIN: 859-669-5987

Applications submitted by mail will be processed within 4 to 6 weeks.

Applications submitted by fax will be processed within 4 business days.

If you have not been notified of your EIN assignment within the normal processing timeframe, please call the IRS Business and Specialty Tax Line at 1-800-829-4933 for assistance.

If you have not received your EIN by the time you need to file a return, write: "Applied For" in the space provided for the EIN.

Avoiding Common EIN Problems

- If you wish to elect to be taxed as an S corporation, you must file Form 2553, Election by a Small Business Corporation (Under Section 1362 of the Internal Revenue Code).

- An association, limited liability company (LLC) or other organization that elects to be taxed as a corporation must file Form 8832, Entity Classification Election.

- Remember to always include your SSN, EIN, or ITIN on Line 7b of Form SS-4.

- Always use the full legal name you entered on Form SS-4, line 1 and the EIN given to you, consistently on all business tax returns you file with the IRS.

- If you change your address and/or you change the responsible party for the entity after you receive your EIN, you must use Form Form 8822-B, Change of Address or Responsible Party - Business, to notify the IRS of the new address.

- If you change your business name after you receive your EIN, write to us at the address where you file your tax return. The request to change your business name must be signed by an authorized person. Additionally, partnerships and corporations must include a copy of the Articles of Amendment that were filed with the state that authorized the name change.

- If the U.S. Postal Service doesn't deliver mail to your street address and you have a P.O. Box, show the P.O. Box number as the entity's mailing address instead of the street address.

www.ingramcontent.com/pod-product-compliance
Lightning Source LLC
Chambersburg PA
CBHW021858170526
45157CB00006B/2500